Remembering My Dad

A Guided Journal To Cherish Our Memories

Barbara L. Mason

INTRODUCTION

I decided to write this book because I want to help
you remember your dad in a very special way
and give you a place to capture your most precious
memories of the time spent with him.

With each page, I have given you a memory prompt
to capture your memories about your dad.
Take one day a week to reflect on the moments you
shared and allow them to bring you to a
place of healing and strength but most of all, a deep
heartfelt gratitude for being able to call him DAD.

With Love and Hope,

Barbara L. Mason

My proudest moment to be his daughter/son was when...

3 words that best describe my dad when
I was growing up are...

When I was younger, I can describe
my dad in these 3 words

_____
_____
_____
_____
_____
_____
_____
_____
_____
_____
_____
_____
_____
_____
_____
_____
_____
_____
_____
_____
_____
_____
_____
_____
_____

Once I became an adult, I would use
these 3 words to describe my dad...

If I had 5 more minutes more with him, I would tell him....

The most special event I wish my dad
could have seen was...

_____
_____
_____
_____
_____
_____
_____
_____
_____
_____
_____
_____
_____
_____
_____
_____
_____
_____
_____
_____
_____
_____
_____
_____
_____

My dad's favorite color was....

The word that best describes my dad's parenting style is....

My friends thought my dad was....

My dad and the kitchen were...

I was so mad at my dad when ....

People say I remind me of my dad when I do...

This made me respect my father so much when...

My dad would want to see me accomplish ....

My dad's fashion statement and
favorite thing to wear was...

The personality trait I have most like my dad is...

I look like my dad by....

My dad's favorite saying when I was in trouble was...

I knew my dad was strong when...

_____ always reminds me of my dad...

The greatest life lesson my dad taught me is....

My funniest memory of my dad is...

I remember a time I was scared and my dad....

_____
_____
_____
_____
_____
_____
_____
_____
_____
_____
_____
_____
_____
_____
_____
_____
_____
_____
_____
_____
_____
_____
_____
_____
_____

How do you want your dad to be
remembered to your kids/others?

I thought my dad was going to kill me when I...

_____

_____
_____
_____
_____
_____
_____
_____
_____
_____
_____
_____
_____
_____
_____
_____
_____
_____
_____
_____
_____
_____
_____
_____
_____

My dad's best advice to me was...

My dad's favorite things to do were...

When my dad would come from work, he would...

The one thing my dad could cook well was...

Inside jokes I had with my dad....

My dad always said this about boys...

My dad always hated when I....

I saw my dad cry when....

My dad's favorite holiday

My dad always wanted to do _____ on his birthday...

_____
_____
_____
_____
_____
_____
_____
_____
_____
_____
_____
_____
_____
_____
_____
_____
_____
_____
_____
_____
_____
_____
_____
_____
_____
_____
_____

My dad's favorite meal was....

_____
_____
_____
_____
_____
_____
_____
_____
_____
_____
_____
_____
_____
_____
_____
_____
_____
_____
_____
_____
_____
_____
_____

My dad always said I did this when I was a baby...

_____
_____
_____
_____
_____
_____
_____
_____
_____
_____
_____
_____
_____
_____
_____
_____
_____
_____
_____
_____
_____
_____
_____

When I was upset, my dad would....

The thing I used to always do with my dad was....

_____

_____

_____

_____

_____

_____

_____

_____

_____

_____

_____

_____

_____

_____

_____

_____

_____

_____

_____

_____

_____

_____

_____

One thing I kept from my dad was...

I wish I could have told my dad...

The one regret I have regarding my dad is....

My dad's favorite game was...

_____
_____
_____
_____
_____
_____
_____
_____
_____
_____
_____
_____
_____
_____
_____
_____
_____
_____
_____
_____
_____
_____
_____

My dad's favorite sport was...

My dad's favorite restaurant was...

The one thing that would make my dad laugh was...

The one thing that my dad would
do to make me laugh was....

My dad made me feel so special when he....

_____
_____
_____
_____
_____
_____
_____
_____
_____
_____
_____
_____
_____
_____
_____
_____
_____
_____
_____
_____
_____
_____
_____
_____

My dad and I's best trip together were...

_____
_____
_____
_____
_____
_____
_____
_____
_____
_____
_____
_____
_____
_____
_____
_____
_____
_____
_____
_____
_____
_____
_____
_____

My dad's favorite thing to wear was...

My dad was disappointed when I...

Best character trait I got from my dad is....

One of the biggest sacrifices my dad
made for our family was...

. . . .

The friend that my dad disliked the most was....

The guy/girl my dad wanted me to marry is...

My dad would always tell me to
_____ when I left the house.

_____

_____

_____

_____

_____

_____

_____

_____

_____

_____

_____

_____

_____

_____

_____

_____

_____

_____

_____

_____

_____

_____

_____

His favorite thing to do on the weekend was...

I have kept _____ to remind me of him

Every time I see/smell/hear _____, I think of my dad

After my dad passed away, it took me the longest to...

I will never forget when my dad said...

The very last memory I have of me and my dad is...

My dad and I would talk on the phone about ......

My dad's favorite sport to watch was...

My dad's favorite room in the house was...

I sound just like my father when I say '_____"...

One of my dad's rules I hated the most was...

_____

_____

_____

_____

_____

_____

_____

_____

_____

_____

_____

_____

_____

_____

_____

_____

_____

_____

_____

_____

_____

_____

_____

_____

_____

The best thing I could do to honor my dad's legacy is....

Made in the USA
Las Vegas, NV
28 September 2023

78280176R00039